Original title:
Timberland Treasures

Copyright © 2025 Creative Arts Management OÜ
All rights reserved.

Author: Ryan Sterling
ISBN HARDBACK: 978-1-80567-367-5
ISBN PAPERBACK: 978-1-80567-666-9

The Music of the Wild

Squirrels dance, a jig so bright,
Chasing tails in morning light.
Birds sing tunes of pure delight,
Critters join the forest fight.

Twirling leaves with whispered breeze,
Bumbles buzzing 'round the trees.
Rabbits hopping 'til they sneeze,
Nature's laughter brings us ease.

Beneath the Starlit Grove

Fireflies twinkle, quite a show,
Dancing shadows, to and fro.
Crickets chirp a song so slow,
Beneath the stars, the night does glow.

Moonlit paths where bobcats prance,
Raccoons plotting their next dance.
Who can catch a glance, perchance,
In this woodland game of chance?

Ferns and Feathers

Ferns do wiggle, quite a sight,
While herons strut, full of delight.
Pine cones fall with all their might,
Making woodland creatures fight.

Owls hoot softly in the night,
While chipmunks giggle, full of fright.
In this tale of fluff and flight,
Nature's stage, a pure delight.

Rustic Echoes of Home

Logs are stacked like waiting guests,
Where raccoons plan their little quests.
Woodpeckers drum, giving their best,
Nature's band, with no time to rest.

Trees whisper secrets, quite absurd,
While squirrels plot; they're never deterred.
In this funny, wild world,
Life's simple joys are pure and blurred.

Reverie Among the Roots

In a forest nook, where the squirrels play,
A fox tells tales of a clumsy jay.
The mushrooms giggle, in their rainbow suits,
While rabbits tap dance in shiny boots.

The old oak leans, he's got some jokes,
About the bear who played with a bunch of folks.
While leaves do the shimmy and branches sway,
Nature's nightclub opens, come what may!

At sunset's kiss, the shadows prance,
Chipmunks are leading a joyful dance.
With acorns thrown, they cheer and shout,
Who knew nature had such a wild bout?

So join the fun, don't be a grouch,
In this leafy realm of whimsy and slouch.
A paradise where laughter is grand,
Among the roots, we take our stand.

The Archive of the Elements

In whispered winds, the stories swirl,
About a sly fox and his leafy pearl.
A wise old tree tipped his hat with flair,
Said, "Pinecones are gold, if you dare to share!"

The river chuckled, skipping rocks in jest,
While birds conducted a giddy fest.
With feathers pinned, they dance through the air,
Storing giggles in clouds, if you care!

Earth grumbled softly, "It's not all clay,
I hide sunshine treasures in piles of hay!"
The rain tapped rhythms, a jolly decree,
"Together we make this giggle spree!"

So venture forth, in the curious green,
Where laughter's the glue that holds it keen.
In the archive of fun, let mischief unite,
Among the elements, everything's right!

Shadows on the Forest Floor

Beneath the trees, where shadows play,
A raccoon finds mischief in broad daylight.
Slinking along with a cheeky grin,
He steals a snack, let the fun begin!

The bunnies laugh, they roll with glee,
Over twigs and roots, wild and free.
With every hop, they shout with pride,
"Who needs a picnic, when chaos is inside?"

A sleepy bear dreams of pies and cake,
While squirrels conspire to launch a shake.
Acorns fly as laughter ignites,
In this playful world, we've got our sights!

So gather 'round, let's not ignore,
The magic beneath the trees we adore.
With shadows dancing and spirits high,
Let's frolic together till the time says goodbye!

Forest Starlight Awakening

When night falls softly, owls start to chat,
Squirrels in pajamas, wearing a hat.
Moonlight dances on branches high,
A raccoon is plotting, oh my, oh my!

Leaves giggle gently, rustling with glee,
The trees whisper secrets, just wait and see.
Fireflies flicker like stars on a dare,
While chipmunks are hosting a wild midnight fair.

The Alchemy of Arbor

In a grove where laughter grows wide,
A tree offers fruit if you tickle its side.
Saplings throw parties, branches swing low,
Dance with the breeze, let your worries go.

Barking up trees, the dogs start to sing,
While frogs in the pond declare it's a fling.
With acorns as confetti, it's quite a sight,
Join the grand revel, it's nature's delight!

Gentle Strength Beneath the Surface

Beneath the thick roots, a party is on,
Mice with top hats perform till the dawn.
Worms in tuxedos discuss politics,
And beetles breakdance, they've got the right mix.

Underneath soil, there's laughter to hear,
A council of critters, they've got no fear.
With every shake of a branch up above,
Nature's slapstick is what they all love.

The Spirit of Nature's Archive

Old logs keep secrets, wise tales to tell,
With a squirrel's great wisdom, all's bound to go well.
The blushing flowers gossip, gossip, they do,
They've seen every folly but keep it in view.

Branches are gossipers, twisting and bending,
Sharing wild rumors of leaves unending.
The birds act as couriers, swift through the trees,
Delivering stories on a whimsical breeze.

Hues of the Whispering Woods

In the woods where squirrels prance,
The trees all wear their leafy pants.
A squirrel steals my sandwich stash,
While the chipmunks laugh and dash.

Frogs croak tunes like a band so grand,
As if they know they're in demand.
A rabbit hops to steal my hat,
And strikes a pose, just like a cat.

The flowers bloom in silly shapes,
All pretending they're escapees from tapes.
The sun peeks through each cloudy float,
As birds argue, riding on a goat.

But when I tread on squeaky twigs,
I wonder why they dance like pigs.
Nature tricks me with its glee,
In this funny place where I feel free.

Reflections by the Rushing Stream

Beside the stream where bubbles sing,
I watch the fish wear tiny bling.
A turtle slowly takes a dive,
While ducks attempt a funny jive.

The water flows like it's in haste,
As beavers gnaw on nature's waste.
A fish jumps out to steal my shoe,
And lands again, like it just knew.

The pebbles giggle as they roll,
Creating laughter, that's their goal.
A frog pretends it's on a stage,
Reciting tales, becoming sage.

I toss a stone with a great splash,
And watch the frogs perform a dash.
Here by the stream, so fresh and bright,
I ponder if they'll join the fight.

Golden Hours in the Greenhouse

Inside the glass where veggies glow,
The cucumbers dance, putting on a show.
Tomatoes blush, just like they're shy,
While peppers wave, a greeting high.

The basil whispers secrets bold,
While thyme tells tales of heroes old.
Yet, hidden there, a gnome so sly,
Winks his eye, just passing by.

In pots, the herbs form quite a crew,
As carrots plot their escape, it's true.
The radishes feel like they're on fire,
While broccoli laughs with leafy choir.

When night descends, they share a laugh,
Debating who gets the first watering half.
In this greenhouse filled with cheer,
I join the fun, I raise a beer.

Lullabies of the Evening Woods

As night falls softly o'er the glade,
The crickets chuckle, serenade.
The owls hoot jokes in rhythmic tune,
While fireflies blink, they're little moons.

Around the trees, the shadows creep,
Even the rocks are trying to sleep.
Bats swoop low in a comic flight,
Through the dark, they joke and bite.

The rustling leaves share silly dreams,
Of acorns sailing down the streams.
A raccoon peers with mischief clear,
Hoping to score a midnight beer.

In this woods where laughter swells,
Each creature's tale magically dwells.
As the night wraps us in its cover,
I giggle softly, under nature's lover.

The Colors of Fall's Farewell

Leaves dance down with glee,
In shades of red and gold.
Squirrels wear tiny hats,
Gathering nuts quite bold.

Pumpkins roll like bowling balls,
In fields of haystack fun.
Scarecrows take a selfie,
And claim they're number one.

Chilly breezes tease the trees,
Who shiver in delight.
A fox slides on fallen leaves,
What a comical sight!

As winter creeps to say hello,
We wave the fall goodbye.
With sweaters and hot cocoa cheer,
We sip as snowflakes fly.

A Journey Through Whispering Woods

In the woods where whispers play,
Trees giggle, leaves applaud.
A raccoon plays peek-a-boo,
While deer just nod and nod.

Bugs wear tiny party hats,
The ants just dance away.
A snail races past with speed,
Rushing to a buffet.

Trees gossip through the breeze,
"Did you hear about the owl?"
They hoot and hoot in fun,
Its wisdom like a growl.

As shadows stretch and darken,
We laugh beneath the stars.
With glowworms lighting paths,
We're kings and queens of bars!

Nature's Silent Keepers

Rocks have stories etched in time,
Secrets whispered low.
Moss makes good soft pillows,
As frogs prepare a show.

A raccoon wears a trench coat,
Pretending it's a spy.
It sips on dew from petals,
Underneath the quiet sky.

Birds gossip on the wire,
About the world below.
With beaks dipped in the chatter,
They cackle, laugh, and go.

As night wraps its dark blanket,
The moon becomes the guide.
Owls hoot their sleepy humor,
While all of nature sighed.

Reflections in the Timber

Puddles mirror the sky's blue,
Where frogs perform a play.
Trees clap their leafy hands,
As nature finds a way.

The creek tickles pebbly feet,
With laughter in each splash.
A beaver's building castles,
Creating quite a splash!

Sunlight winks through branches,
Painting patterns on the ground.
A chipmunk sings a jingle,
While dancing all around.

As twilight paints the drama,
With hues of pink and gray,
Nature's a stand-up comic,
In its own funny way.

The Lore of the Leafy Canopy

In a forest filled with glee,
Squirrels dance on branches free.
They wear tiny hats quite neat,
And challenge us to a nutty treat.

The owls gossip in the trees,
In their robes, they're sure to please.
Foxes playing hide and seek,
Their laughter echoes through the creek.

Mushrooms hold a secret rave,
With fairies dancing, quite the wave.
They sing songs of morning light,
While rabbits join the silly flight.

And when the sun begins to set,
A raccoon pulls a silly bet.
"Who can swing from that tall vine?"
The forest cheers, it's quite divine!

Enchantment of the Timber Trails

On trails where laughter lingers,
Frogs wear shoes and dance with fingers.
They leap around in funny ways,
And avoid those muddy sprays.

A porcupine plays hide and seek,
"Guess my quills!" he shouts, so cheek.
But everyone just runs away,
Who wants a prickly game, I say?

The paths are lined with giggles sweet,
As chipmunks race on tiny feet.
They carry snacks much bigger than
Their little paws can ever span.

And when the sun dips low and red,
The fireflies light up their bed.
Glow in the dark, they'll start to twirl,
In this enchanted, silly world!

Where the Wild Things Grow

In a place where wild things bloom,
Bunnies wield a giant broom.
They sweep the leaves with much delight,
While birds sing from morning to night.

Dancing flowers wink and sway,
Swaying in a humorous play.
Bees don tuxedos, buzzing loud,
Attracting butterflies, quite proud.

A bear attempts a silly dance,
Twisting, tumbling, takes a chance.
He slips on berries, what a sight!
The forest roars in pure delight.

And as the stars begin to shine,
The critters share a glass of brine.
They toast to laughter, joy, and cheer,
For in this wild, there's nothing to fear!

The Earth Beneath the Branches

Under branches, snug and low,
Worms wear sunglasses, steal the show.
They wiggle dance in rhythm, fast,
Whispering secrets of the past.

Ants march home with tiny spoons,
Collecting snacks like little loons.
They giggle at their burdens vast,
"Just one more crumb, let's make it last!"

A hedgehog spins a wheel of fun,
Rolls over roots, he's on the run.
He claims he's training for a race,
But honestly, it's just a silly chase.

As night descends and shadows creep,
The earth holds dreams, both wide and deep.
So gather 'round, and hear the lore,
Beneath the branches, life's never a bore!

A Treetop Reverie

Up high where squirrels dance and prance,
Birds argue over their fancy pants,
The sun peeks through the leafy holes,
While ants hold meetings to plan their roles.

A hammock swings with a lazy grin,
As I snack on acorns, chucking the skin,
The breeze whispers secrets in playful tones,
While woodpeckers tap out their funny drones.

The branches sway like a wobbly boat,
A chipmunk in a hat steals the showboat,
Laughing at nature's odd parade,
As frolicking critters play romantic charades.

So join the fun in the leafy maze,
Where everyone's smiling in curious ways,
Let's flip our worries to the breeze,
And laugh with the leaves, oh pretty please!

Beneath the Boughs

Beneath the branches, shadows do flip,
As rabbits debate on their latest trip,
A turtle walks slow, with a pom-pom crew,
While a friendly frog croaks, 'Let's start a zoo!'

The scent of pine fills the air, it's true,
But who forgot to bring the afternoon stew?
The trees all chuckle, their branches jive,
While a raccoon juggles, trying to thrive.

Laughter echoes in the forest deep,
Where the chipmunks giggle and never sleep,
A squirrel in shades gives the latest scoop,
While berries fall like confetti, what a loop!

So waddle here, and join the fun,
Underneath the boughs, where we're never done,
For in this woodland where smiles abound,
Laughter and joy are forever found.

Nature's Forgotten Symphony

In the woods, an orchestra plays quite the tune,
With a chorus of birds that croon at high noon,
A badger conducts with a root for a stick,
As the breeze joins in, giggling quick!

The flowers sway side to side, in delight,
While the sunbeams dance and twirl in flight,
Critters gather for the grand debut,
With insects on strings, making a crew.

The drumming of woodpeckers keeps the beat,
While turtles tango with two left feet,
A caterpillar solo, oh what a sight,
As hedgehogs hum under soft moonlight.

So gather 'round for this odd ballet,
As nature's jesters have much to say,
A show full of giggles, a fanciful scheme,
In melodies made of silly, sweet dreams!

Life Between the Leafy Layers

In leafy layers, life sways and hums,
As chattering chipmunks invite all the fun,
A squirrel misjudges when leaping for nuts,
Landing in moss, surrounded by ruts.

The sunlight sprinkles like playful confetti,
While snakes in shadows dance oh-so-frettily,
Mice make plans with giggles and shrieks,
Finding the funniest hide-and-seek peaks.

Under green canopies, creatures unite,
To share witticisms, and take flight,
With whispers of giggles and laughter so sweet,
As ladybugs wear tiny red feet.

So let's stroll through layers of green and gold,
Where each little critter's a story retold,
For in this grand place, hilarity flows,
And life's little treasures are everyone's shows!

Echoes in the Hollow

In the hollow, a goat sings,
Wearing a hat made of twigs.
He dances like nobody's watching,
While crickets play the jigs.

Squirrels laugh in the trees,
Juggling acorns with flair.
One drops his prize on my head,
Oh, the nutty despair!

A rabbit hops in a bow tie,
With style that can't be beat.
He says, 'Join my fancy dance!'
I trip over my feet.

The wise old owl says to me,
'Why not join in the fun?'
I reply, 'Only if you sing,
Or I might just run!'

Ribbons of Sunlight in the Brambles

Sunlight weaves through the thorns,
Like ribbons in a game.
A hedgehog rolls in laughter,
As I try to do the same.

Bumblebees buzz a tune,
One lands on my nose with glee.
I sneeze and twirl like a dancer,
Bees scatter, buzzing 'Flee!'

The thistles start a debate,
'Who's the prickliest of them all?'
They poke and tease each other,
Until they all start to ball.

In the bramble ball pit, oh dear,
Everyone starts to bounce.
We giggle till we tumble down,
While the fox just pouts and pounce.

Whispers of the Woodland Creatures

The fox whispered right to the mole,
'Your burrow's quite a sight!'
The mole popped up with a grin,
'You should try it—it's just right!'

A raccoon wore a mask of dirt,
Claimed he was the bandit king.
We all chuckled at his charm,
And joined him in a swing!

The deer were laughing at a tree,
That seemed to bend and sway.
They said, 'Look at the old oak dance,
He thinks it's his birthday today!'

And who knew the turtle could breakdance?
In his shell, he starts to spin.
With each slow turn and a shuffle,
We all cheer, 'Wow, go win!'

The Pulse of Pine Needles

The pines rustle like gossip,
As they sway in the breeze.
A porcupine teaches the rhythm,
'Tickles? No, not these!'

Branches bounce with the laughter,
As needles hit the ground.
A skunk joins in with a jig,
His scent a friend profound.

The woodland shakes with each step,
A dance-off underway!
The toads croak out their applause,
As mushrooms cheer, 'Hooray!'

Roots twist in wild confusion,
'Which way do we spin?'
As I fall flat on my belly,
The forest shouts, 'Let's begin!'

The Elder's Whisper

In the woods where squirrels play,
An old tree grumbles every day.
"Who stole my acorns?" it cried aloud,
While birds just laughed, oh how they bowed.

A raccoon with a mischievous grin,
Stashed snacks where the branches thin.
"What's in the basket?" the chipmunk frets,
"Just leftovers from last night's best bets!"

Moss-covered logs hold secrets tight,
While owls hoot jokes in soft moonlight.
Every rustle seems to bring a jest,
Nature's punchlines are truly the best.

So if you hear the forest giggle,
Join in the fun, give a little wiggle.
Amidst the trees, where laughter roams,
Even the roots feel right at home!

Gems of the Green Domain

Amidst the ferns and leafy flair,
A squirrel finds gems beyond compare.
"Are those my nuts or just shiny rocks?"
It chuckles loud, ignoring the clocks.

Beneath the branches, a rabbit leaps,
In search of carrots, it quietly creeps.
But what's that glimmer? A silver spoon!
"For my tea with the stars?" it asked the moon.

The brook babbles with a bubbling joke,
Tickling feet of the sleeping oak.
"Here comes the sun, let's play hide and seek!"
As leaves burst forth, each one unique.

In this realm, the wild things jest,
Nature holds its laughter, the very best.
With every step, adventures unfold,
In a world where treasures are happily bold!

Portrait of the Silent Grove

In a grove where the trees stand tall,
A painter's brush gives nature a call.
"What's this? A portrait of my old branch?"
The whispers tease, as leaves do a dance.

A badger scurries, set for a show,
In polka-dot pants, with a vibrant bow.
"Why the long face?" asks the blushing bee,
"Just trying to look extra fancy, see?"

A beetle hums while balancing treats,
Pinecones and berries, oh what a feat!
"I'm the star of this woodland stage,"
The tree bark chuckles, filled with sage.

Meanwhile, shadows play tricks on light,
As fireflies flicker, igniting the night.
In this silent grove, there's always cheer,
Nature's gallery, full of mirth and dear!

Secrets of the Bark and Bough

In the nooks of bark, odd tales reside,
With squirrels eavesdropping, filled with pride.
A woodpecker knocks, a rhythmic tune,
Painting secrets with a crescent moon.

The merry raccoons hold a grand feast,\nWith leftovers
from the last week's beast.
"Is that lasagna?" the crow caws loud,
While all around, laughter forms a crowd.

Upon the boughs, the shadows play,
As frogs croak jokes in their own way.
"Have you heard about the snail race?"
Slow and steady, in their own space.

So listen close when the forest talks,
In the rustling leaves and the scampering walks.
Nature's humor, in every nook,
Equals a chapter in the best storybook!

Veins of Life Flowing

In the woods where squirrels race,
Trees have hugs, and nature's grace.
A raccoon with a mask so neat,
Tiptoes lightly on his feet.

Beneath a branch, an acorn rolls,
The wind tells tales, and laughter trolls.
A chipmunk's dance, so quick and spry,
As tiny ants march close, oh my!

From bugs to blooms, a busy scene,
Who makes the best pie? The hedgehog queen!
She whirls and twirls, a kitchen star,
Striving to bake like a woodland czar.

Nature giggles, a soft delight,
Every creature, a comical sight.
In the heart of these vibrant lands,
Joy spills over from nature's hands.

Mossy Tales of the Glade

In a glade where mushrooms bloom,
Fungi gossip, a fragrant plume.
Toadstools gather, sipping dew,
"Did you hear? A snail flew too!"

A wise old owl shares his dreams,
Of pizza crusts and melting creams.
With goofy owlets in tow,
"Let's make a pie, let's steal the show!"

Moss blankets floors like thick, green wool,
While armored beetles strut and pull.
"Guard your snacks, my friends!" they yell,
"Or ants will form a marching cell!"

In laughter's arms, the day slips by,
As flowers giggle; bees all sigh.
Nature's jokes, a joyful face,
In this lush, enchanting place.

Sunlight Dances on Leaves

Sunlight winks amid the trees,
Leaves shimmy as if to tease.
A butterfly in polka dots,
Stumbles on a group of tots.

"Catch me if you can!" it flirts,
While caterpillars munch on shirts.
A playful breeze begins to swirl,
Sending leaves into a twirl.

Beneath a branch, a rabbit grins,
Wearing glasses; it surely wins.
"Who's got the best carrot stew?
I dare you to taste my secret brew!"

Joy spills forth in golden beams,
As the forest sings and dreams.
In dances of the sun's warm glow,
Nature's humor steals the show.

Shadows of Giants

In the shade of giants' limbs,
Little critters dance and whim.
A fox who thinks he's quite a beast,
Adopts the role of forest priest.

Squirrels chatter secrets tight,
About the owl's late-night flight.
"Did he spot anything to eat?
Or just a worm who's lost his seat?"

With shadows long, the sun dips low,
A clever raccoon steals the show.
"This earth is mine!" he claims with glee,
While juggling nuts and climbing a tree.

Laughter echoes, soft and sweet,
As forest friends share tales to greet.
In shadows cast by nature's hand,
Life's funny biz is always planned.

Beauty in Decay

Once was a tree so proud and tall,
Now it droops and has no gall.
Squirrels dance on branches bare,
Laughing at the lack of hair.

Mushrooms sprout, a quirky sight,
Holding court with glee at night.
A snappy vine tied up my shoe,
I guess it thinks it's funny too!

Leaves drift down, a waltz they prance,
Nature's way of throwing a chance.
While woodpeckers knock and peck,
We giggle at the tree's great wreck.

So here's to laughs in nature's guise,
Even in endings, humor flies.
Let's toast to roots that turned to dust,
And find the charm in all that rust.

Echoes of the Forest Heart

In a forest deep, the echoes play,
Whispers of leaves that dance and sway.
A woodchuck chuckled, what a sound!
His antics made me spin around.

Birds chirped loud, a raucous choir,
One even tried to start a fire!
With acorns flying, oh what a show,
Who knew woods had such a glow?

Frogs croaked jokes from ponds of green,
Telling tales of sights unseen.
A raccoon grinned with pie on its face,
As if this was the prime of grace.

Each tree has a tale, a laugh in disguise,
Where shadows and sunlight blend and rise.
Let's tell our stories, bold and bright,
For laughter echoes long into the night.

Chronicles of the Woodland Spirits

The sprites in the woods play tricks galore,
Hiding in ferns, behind nature's door.
With big wide eyes and a silly grin,
They tie up the squirrels, it's all in good fun!

One fairy fumbled while dusting a leaf,
Tripped over moss, oh what a grief!
While giggling goblins, small and spry,
Made friends with a beetle, oh my, oh my!

They launch pine cones with all their might,
A glorious dodgeball in the fading light.
And if you listen on a quiet day,
You'll hear their laughter echo and play.

Woodland spirits, small yet bold,
Weave a tapestry of joy untold.
Let's join their shenanigans and cheer,
For whimsy abounds when nature's here!

Treasures Caught in Sunlight

A glimmering pebble on the forest floor,
Looks just like gold, can't ask for more!
But wait, it's just a darkened stone,
Still, it shines bright, a king on its throne.

Spider webs trap the morning dew,
Glittering jewels in the forest's view.
A bird lands, it's no royal guest,
Tries to steal shiny things, but it's truly a jest.

A log with worms, who knew their worth?
Nature's own gold beneath the earth!
A snail slides by, its shell a delight,
Laughing at treasures, lost out of sight.

So wander these woods, grab joy by the bunch,
See the wonders, laugh much as you crunch.
In every nook, there's fun to unfold,
In the forest of treasure, where stories are told.

The Art of Natural Abundance

In the forest's heart, squirrels play,
Gathering nuts in a comical way.
With acorn hats and tiny feet,
They dance around, the forest's beat.

Beneath the pines, a rabbit hops,
Thinking he's found some ginger tops.
But wait a sec, it's just a weed,
He pauses, then he takes the lead!

A bear rolls over, tumbling round,
Searching for snacks he thinks he found.
But alas! It's just an empty can,
He shrugs it off, a busy man.

The birds above, in goofy flight,
Chirp out jokes, oh what a sight!
With laughter ringing, all around,
Nature's fun can truly astound.

Awakening the Canopy's Spirit

The trees all whisper tales in jest,
Of leaves that tickle, at their best.
A squirrel chuckles, 'Look at me!'
As he slips down, a vibrant spree.

A raccoon sneaks, with mischief planned,
In search of snacks, he's got a hand.
But all he finds are muddy boots,
He grins, and wobbles in his roots.

The owls hoot, giving wise advice,
'Play it cool, and roll the dice!'
A little dance on branches high,
Makes everyone laugh, oh my, oh my!

Breezes tease the branches tall,
Making them sway, a nature sprawl.
In a world where laughter reigns,
Joyful moments among the chains.

Secrets Among the Firs

In a grove where secrets stay,
Pinecones giggle, at their play.
Shadows hide, with cuddly smiles,
Tickling toes for endless miles.

The chipmunks chatter, full of cheer,
Swapping tales that are quite queer.
One lost his lunch, oh what a shame,
Now every nut's a new found game!

Underneath a mossy throne,
A frog croaks out a funny tone.
He sings of flies in a grand ballet,
While hiding from the sun's bright ray.

As twilight falls, the stars take flight,
Creatures gather for the night.
With tales of fun, the forest glows,
Mysteries shared where laughter flows.

The March of the Meadow

In the meadow, a parade begins,
Butterflies dance, sparking grins.
Grasshoppers leap with jumps so high,
While daisies nod and wave goodbye.

A deer prances, strutting proud,
Saying, 'Look at me!' to the crowd.
But tripping on a hidden root,
He flips, landing in a leafy suit.

The ants march on, in perfect line,
One lost his lunch—said he'd be fine.
They all break dance, and start to groove,
A tiny party with a silly move!

As sunlight dips, the crickets chirp,
Playing tunes that make you burp.
The meadow's fun, with joy and cheer,
Reminds us all, laughter's near.

The Lure of Leafy Labyrinths

In the woods where squirrels play,
Leaves like hats during the day.
A twist, a turn, then a sneeze,
Was that a branch or just some bees?

Rabbits hop with stylish flair,
Making friends with woodland air.
But watch your step, it's quite a game,
I tripped on roots and felt some shame!

Mushrooms giggle, trees stand tall,
Nature's giggles over all.
Chasing shadows, dodging light,
Who knew woods could be this bright?

Yet on the path, my snack was found,
A raccoon's giggle, oh so round.
He took my sandwich, what a cheek,
In leafy mazes, laughter's peak!

Nature's Hidden Alchemy

In the forest where magic brews,
Mushrooms dance in polka shoes.
The owls wear glasses, wise and chic,
Conspiring secrets we can't peek!

Lost in bushes, a wizard's hat,
With sparkly stones, look at that!
The rabbits brew their herbal tea,
While foxes rhyme beneath the tree.

Tall oaks whisper secrets loud,
Like quirky uncles in a crowd.
A crow croaks puns with glee each day,
While animals join the silly play!

Nature's alchemy, oh so grand,
With laughter echoing through the land.
From bark to berry, jokes unfold,
In this wild realm, that can't be sold!

The Spirit of the Old Growth

Beneath the ancient, creaky boughs,
Where trees stand strong, like ancient cows.
The squirrels tell tales from long ago,
Of legends lost in the forest's glow.

A raccoon with a crafty grin,
Picks up the nuts that he did win.
While deer break dance in the moonlight's gleam,
Their antlers shine, like some wild dream!

The old growth laughs with every breeze,
Tickling leaves, it aims to please.
Whimsy swirls in the purple mist,
Who knew nature could do such a twist?

So raise your glass to ancient trees,
Who share their jokes with playful ease.
Each ring a story, each knot a cheer,
In this old haven, full of weird!

Harmony of the Timbered Realm

In the timbered realm where shadows dance,
A bear rides tricycles, what a chance!
With trees that giggle, flowers that smile,
This forest is quirky, stay for a while!

Woodpeckers drum in a band so bold,
Playing rhythms of secrets untold.
The fox struts by with his fancy scarf,
Cracking jokes that make the owls laugh!

A stream flows gently, singing a tune,
About a frog who stuck to the moon.
With every splash, delight's abound,
Nature's jesters springing around!

So join the fun in this leafy space,
With woodland creatures filled with grace.
In harmony, they leap and twirl,
In this dreamlike, timbered world!

Beneath the Bark's Embrace

Squirrels plot their daring heists,
While raccoons throw their wild feast nights.
The owls hoot at midnight's scene,
Creating chaos, quite unseen.

The tough bark hides such giggles grand,
With secrets whispered 'cross the land.
A beetle wears his finest suit,
To crash the party, oh what a hoot!

Trees giggle as the branches sway,
Living their lives in their own way.
The roots establish underground fun,
While frogs serenade the setting sun.

In this realm where laughter grows,
Among the flowers, nobody knows,
That underneath the bark's soft shade,
Fortunes of folly proudly parade.

Glimmers of the Gnarled Branches

Gnarled branches twist like silly straws,
As wise old trees just laugh and pause.
With every twist, a secret shared,
In their humor, none are spared.

Funky mushrooms dance in a ring,
To the chorus that the crickets sing.
The sun sneezes through leaves on high,
While tiny birds aim for the sky.

Nature's circus, a lovely sight,
With tumbleweeds in playful flight.
The shadows stretch, a playful tease,
In the realms of uproarious trees.

All around, the spirit's bold,
Adventures waiting to unfold.
With glimmers of laughter in their sash,
Even the wind joins in for a crash!

A Dance with the Windblown Leaves

Leaves twirl in a windy ballet,
While squirrels are the star of the day.
They chatter, jump, and swing about,
Caught up in a rhythmic shout.

The gusts play tag with every tree,
As branches bend and twist with glee.
A dance-off starts in nature's hall,
Where laughter echoes, embracing all.

Amidst the whirl of colors bright,
The leaves spin like kites in flight.
With every rustle, secrets spill,
As woodland creatures laugh at will.

Join this fest, let spirits lift,
In the glade where nature's gift.
For in this dance with playful ease,
We'll spin and twirl among the trees.

Legends in the Log

A wise old log declared with pride,
Of legends passed from side to side.
With stories whispered night and day,
In a comic twist, they find their way.

The rabbits giggle at the tales,
Of bloopers made by clumsy snails.
The foxes strut, their bravado grand,
While beavers laugh, a stick in hand.

Each notch and groove tells jokes of yore,
Where critters laugh and spirits soar.
With acorns bouncing, laughter spills,
In this log of thrill and silly thrills.

So gather 'round, let humor flow,
In the forest where the legends grow.
For in this timber home of dreams,
True joy is found, or so it seems.

The Heartbeat of the Wildwood

In the forest, squirrels play,
Stealing acorns every day.
Chasing shadows, laughing loud,
They're the jesters of the crowd.

Trees gossip in the breeze,
Whispering secrets to the bees.
The owls debate who's the wisest,
While rabbits claim to be the fastest.

A moose dons a bowler hat,
Strutting by like a suave cat.
Frogs wear tiny polka dots,
Croaking tunes on lily spots.

Beneath the moon, the crickets sing,
Dreaming of their dated fling.
The woods alive with funny quirks,
A wild world where laughter lurks.

Spells of the Leafy Grove

In the leafy grove they dance,
Mice in tuxes, a silly prance.
Toadstool tables, tea they pour,
Inviting all the critters' lore.

A raccoon with a magician's wand,
Making berries vanish, oh so grand.
A spell of giggles, who knew?
They levitate a spoon or two.

Lizards wearing funky shades,
Sunbathing in light cascades.
Frogs cast spells to make friends cheer,
Creating laughter far and near.

Mushrooms laugh, they trip and fall,
While gnomes have their annual ball.
A forest party, never bleak,
With silly spells that make you squeak.

A Canvas of Bark and Petals

The trees paint stories in their bark,
With lines so witty, leaving a mark.
Petals giggle in the gentle breeze,
Crafting art that's sure to tease.

A painter beetle on a thrill,
With colors that will give you a chill.
He paints the flowers in neon hues,
While butterflies flaunt their fashion views.

The grass tickles our toes in play,
As ladybugs guide the way.
With every step, a giggling sound,
A canvas broken, laughter found.

In this garden, hilarity reigns,
With flowering jokes and silly chains.
Nature's brush strokes laugh and blend,
A vibrant masterpiece, no end.

Symphony of the Swaying Branches

Branches sway in a quirky dance,
While critters join in with a chance.
Squirrels spinning like a top,
While the wise old owl can't stop.

A symphony of rustling leaves,
Plays where a playful raccoon weaves.
With every twirl, the breezes hum,
Giving life to every drum.

The bouncy bees conduct the sound,
As hoppy frogs leap all around.
A melody of crazy fun,
In this raucous, wild-run sun.

The giggling branches, nature's stage,
Live out loud, let laughter engage.
A concert where the wildwoods play,
In a silly, joyous ballet!

Beneath the Otherworldly Canopy

In the woods where the shadows play,
Squirrels dance at the break of day.
They wear tiny hats and scurry about,
Chasing each other with giggles and shout.

The trees whisper jokes we can't quite hear,
Branches waving like they have no fear.
A raccoon strolls by with a swagger so wide,
He thinks he's the king of this leafy slide.

The Fabric of Flora

Petals in a quilt, all colors and hues,
Blooming with laughter, wearing their shoes.
Daisies knitting sweaters for ants on the run,
While bees buzz tunes, oh what fun!

The ferns tell secrets in hushed, leafy tones,
As gnomes play croquet with whimsical cones.
Mushrooms giggle, their caps in a spin,
They patter with joy, come join in the din!

Twilight in the Enchanted Grove

When the sun dips low, and the laughter grows,
Fireflies wear capes, don't you know?
They zip and they zoom, in a joyful race,
Lighting up the night, oh what a place!

A wise old owl hoots with a chuckle and wink,
"Don't trip on the roots, or you might sink!"
With fairies on swings made of silk and dreams,
The stars wink back, or so it seems.

Portraits of the Gnarled Old Ones

Ancient trees with faces so grand,
Catch the giggles that float through the land.
They tell silly tales of a long-ago time,
With bark that laughs and moss that rhymes.

Their roots stretch deep, but their humor is light,
Casting shadows and jokes as day turns to night.
A squirrel's deep chuckle sets all in good cheer,
While the owls applaud with a hoot and a leer.

Hidden Gems of the Green

In the forest deep, there's a stash,
Where squirrels plans their silly bash.
With acorns stacked and nuts galore,
They dance around, they can't ignore.

A raccoon thinks he's quite the thief,
He's stealing snacks like it's his grief.
But when found out, he makes a dash,
Tripping over roots in a comical flash.

Mushrooms sprout like silly hats,
While birds sing tunes that sound like chats.
Bouncing bunnies hop with glee,
In this wild show, they're all so free.

But watch your step, or you might slip,
On muddy trails, you'll lose your grip.
With laughter echoing through the air,
Hidden gems are everywhere!

Roots and Reveries

The trees whisper tales of delight,
Of foxes prancing under moonlight.
With roots that twist like silly jokes,
They tickle the toes of passing folks.

A deer tries to play hide and seek,
But behind a bush, it's far too meek.
With branches swaying, they giggle and sway,
While critters frolic and join the play.

A hammock swings where dreams collide,
With sleepy bugs and a lazy slide.
As ants parade with tiny flags,
The party grows, it never drags.

In the heart of the woods, oh what a sight,
Every shadow glows with pure delight.
Through roots and reveries, laughter's near,
Join in the fun, your friends are here!

The Heartbeat of the Earth

Beneath our feet, the ground does thrum,
With beetles drumming a catchy strum.
The Earth's own pulse in giggles rings,
As flowers dance and garden swings.

The rocks all laugh, they're quite a bunch,
With silly faces that guide our lunch.
They tell the tales of days gone by,
Of dragons soaring through the sky.

Bubbles of laughter rise like streams,
Winding through our wildest dreams.
A ticklish breeze whispers your name,
As every leaf plays a funny game.

In every stone, a joke to score,
A fluttering laugh upon the floor.
Feel the rhythm, don't look away,
Join Mother Earth in her playful sway!

Canopy of Dreams

High above in the leafy maze,
Where sunlight peeks in playful rays.
A squirrel's circus is in full swing,
With acrobats leaping, what joy they bring!

A parrot sings a wobbly tune,
While monkeys dance under the moon.
Each branch a stage for wild acts,
As laughter erupts, and joy distracts.

With clouds as pillows, dreams take flight,
In the canopy's heart, everything's right.
The breeze carries giggles from high above,
Wrapping the woods in a blanket of love.

So let's climb up and join the crew,
In a world where the silly feels brand new.
Under this canvas, let's play and schemes,
In our joyous, leafy canopy of dreams!

Grace of the Mossy Floor

Beneath my feet, the moss does spring,
It giggles softly, oh the joy it brings!
With every step, it tickles my toes,
I laugh aloud, where silliness flows.

A dance I do on this soft, green mat,
Dodging squirrels, while I chase my hat.
The moss winks back, a jolly prank,
I swear it's plotting in its spongy rank.

A frog jumps out with a leap and splash,
'Excuse me, human!'—what a funny clash!
I bow and shake my head in glee,
"Mossy floor, you're the life of the spree!"

As I twirl and whirl, it sways and bends,
Our joyous waltz, where the laughter blends.
In this green playground, I find my charm,
A giggly realm, so snug and warm!

Shadows of the Majestic Pines

Under the pines, where shadows play,
I stumble and trip in a comedic way.
They chuckle softly, those towering friends,
Their whispers echo, 'Who'll laugh in the ends?'

A squirrel gives chase, with acorn in tow,
My high-stepping legs make a comical show.
The shade wraps around like a funny cloak,
In this forest theatre, I'm the joke!

The branches sway, trying not to snicker,
While I make faces that could hardly flicker.
A twig snaps loudly—oh what a roar!
'Is that an owl or just me on the floor?'

In this shadowed ballroom, with trees in line,
I spin and twirl, feeling quite fine.
The pines and I, a comic troupe,
Making merry joy in this evergreen loop!

Fables of the Fallen Bark

Scattered about, the bark tells tales,
Of brave little bugs and their funny gales.
As I step on one, it giggles loud,
Echoing stories, funny and proud.

A snail crawls by with a dramatic flair,
'You'll never catch me!' it shouts in the air.
I roll my eyes at its sluggish chase,
'Oh dear snail, you've lost the race!'

Mice in the shadows plot cheeky schemes,
'Let's prank the human, or so it seems!'
I trip on grass as they squeak and dart,
'Is this a fable, or just a good start?'

In a world of laughs and silly delights,
The fallen bark whispers through days and nights.
Every squeal and giggle a treasure unspoken,
In the forest of fables, laughter's never broken!

Aroma of the Forest Floor

The scent of pine is quite the tease,
It tickles my nose and makes me sneeze!
Mushrooms pop up like hats of delight,
I can't help but giggle at this funny sight.

Fungi growing with a humorous twist,
On this funky floor, how can I resist?
Sprinkling spores like confetti in air,
"Join the fun!" they seem to declare.

The earthy blend aches for moments of cheer,
As I stomp about, with laughter sincere.
The aroma whispers, funky and bright,
The forest floor's joy, my pure delight!

With each breath of this charming bouquet,
I trip on a root, laughing all the way.
Aromatic giggles fill up the glade,
In the laughter of nature, I find my parade!

Whispers of the Woodland

Squirrels dance with acorn hats,
Wearing boots of leafy sprats.
Trees chuckle in the sun's embrace,
As rabbits hop with comical grace.

Frogs in ties, so finely dressed,
Leap about for their bequest.
Mice with cheese are on a quest,
In this woodland, they're the best!

Birds gossip with a feathered flair,
Trading tales of what they dare.
Bouncing berries, a berry game,
"Who's the juiciest?" all claim fame.

Sunlight winks through branches high,
While chipmunks giggle as they fly.
A forest filled with breezy cheer,
Bringing smiles through every year.

Secrets Beneath the Canopy

Beneath the leaves, a secret's told,
With dancing mushrooms, brave and bold.
Wiggly worms in suits of dirt,
Tap-dance while the roots convert.

Bunnies gather for a tea,
With acorn cups and all the glee.
While owls hoot with a wise old grin,
"What's the real joke?" they all chime in.

A fox in shades, so astute,
Chasing shadows in a suit.
The streams are giggling, bubbling bright,
As fish plot parties, quite a sight!

With a whisper, leaves collide,
As beetles roll on the fun fair ride.
Secrets rustle, laughter loud,
Nature's mischief, lively crowd!

Echoes of Ancient Pines

Old pines share their ancient lore,
With grumpy crows, who always soar.
"Have you heard of the flying cat?"
They caw together, just imagine that!

Squirrels built a library here,
Filled with tales of yesteryear.
Reading nuts is quite the feat,
With every crack, you can't be beat!

The shadows dance as breezes tease,
While gophers play, just like you please.
A jolly bear, with hat askew,
Sings opera while the ants coo.

Echoes linger, tales unfold,
Of woodland madness, bright and bold.
Laughter trails the paths they roam,
In these woods, they find a home.

Dewy Mornings in the Forest

Morning dew, like jewels bright,
Wakes up critters, oh what a sight!
Frogs in slippers, stretching wide,
Ready to take the day in stride.

Mice in cloaks stroll down the path,
Snickering at the sun's warm bath.
"Let's race to the blueberry patch!"
They giggle, ready for a match.

Hawks on high play peek-a-boo,
With dancing leaves, they steal the view.
Pinecones roll with a cheeky spin,
As forest friends gather in.

Dewy mornings, sparkle bright,
Join the fun, it feels so right.
In this giggling woodlands' play,
Every creature brightens the day.

Secrets of the Woodland

In the woods, a squirrel prances,
Hiding acorns, taking chances.
He thinks he's got a grand design,
But he's lost half of his stash, oh my!

A raccoon peeks with mischievous eyes,
Stealing snacks, a clever disguise.
His friends all laugh at his silly quest,
Food's never safe, he's quite the pest!

Butterflies giggle as they flit and fly,
They tease the ants who march by and by.
"Where's the party?" the buzzing bees hum,
As the woodland bursts into silly fun!

The trees whisper tales of past mischief,
Of owls wearing hats and chipmunks as thieves.
In this jolly glade, where laughter's free,
Nature's comedy, a sight to see!

Embrace of the Evergreen

In the lush green, there's laughter abound,
A pinecone sways, makes a soft sound.
It dreams of being a mighty tree,
While squirrels ride it like a wild spree!

Beneath the branches, a fox takes a nap,
Unaware of the prank by a humorous chap.
A crow drops a twig on his sleepy head,
Wakes him up, and off he fled!

The ferns do a jig, a dance of delight,
While crickets croon songs into the night.
The moon laughs too, casting a grin,
As creatures of night join in the din!

Amidst the trees, the tales unfold,
Of friendships warmed and laughter bold.
In this embracing grove of green cheer,
The jokes of nature echo clear!

The Song of the Silent Trees

Deep in silence, the trees they stand,
Whispering secrets, quite unplanned.
A gust of wind brings a chuckle or two,
As leaves gossip, causing quite a hullabaloo!

The wise old oak, with branches wide,
Shares tales of critters who can't bide.
A bear tried to dance, and oh what a sight,
He tripped on roots, and ran in a fright!

A wandering stream joins in the song,
Laughing at fish who just don't belong.
They flail and splash, then dart away,
Hiding their giggles without delay!

The silent trees hold jokes untold,
Witnessing antics, both silly and bold.
In nature's theater, the laughter runs free,
Life's funny moments, beneath every tree.

Mysteries in the Underbrush

In the underbrush, where shadows play,
A hedgehog ponders, just lying in hay.
He thinks he's invisible, oh such a dream,
As a rabbit pops by, ready to scheme!

A turtle, slow with wisdom to share,
Wonders why deer don't have a care.
They leap and frolic without a fright,
While he's got an agenda—sneaking a bite!

The ants are busy with their silly march,
Forming a line, like they're in a parade thrash.
Then one trips over, falls in a spin,
They all look back and laugh with a grin!

In this world of fun beneath the leaves,
Where creatures play tricks, and no one grieves.
Mysteries dwell in this lively brush,
With giggles and chuckles—a joyful hush!

During the Dusk's Embrace

In the woods where the silliness roams,
Squirrels chat while reciting poems.
They trip on acorns, giggle with glee,
Nature's comedians, wild and free.

Bouncing branches, they give a wave,
A raccoon shows off his dance like a brave.
He fumbles and tumbles on mossy ground,
Laughter echoes, a joyful sound.

Even the owls wear tiny hats,
With spectacles perched, oh, how they chat!
Starlight winks through leafy skies,
As everyone shares the silliest lies.

Chasing shadows, they play peek-a-boo,
A game of tag with a sly chipmunk crew.
At dusk, the forest becomes a stage,
A comedy show, all engaged!

The Songbird's Serenade

A parrot in a bow tie sings with flair,
While blue jays laugh, dancing in the air.
With wobbly notes, they try to impress,
A fancy concert, but it's quite a mess.

Chirping crickets join in the fun,
Their rhythm stutters, then they run.
A note gone wrong, a zany show,
The bushes tremble with laughter's flow.

Canaries trip over their own tune,
While mockingbirds croon beneath the moon.
The trees shake with all their chatter,
In this wild realm, nothing's the matter.

With feathery friends, it's a raucous game,
Each one trying to outdo the same.
Nature's musicians, silly as can be,
Their symphony born from pure glee.

Flicker of Fireflies

Fireflies flicker with a bug's delight,
Playing tag in the warm summer night.
With lanterns bright, they dance and sway,
Casting shadows in a playful way.

A glowworm grins with a soft, sly light,
He thinks he's the star of the buzzing night.
But tripping over grass, he fumbles and flips,
Leaving a trail of giggles and quips.

A moth arrives, fancy as a cape,
But flapping wings become an escape.
He spirals and twirls, a comedy king,
In the midst of this shimmering bling.

The night is alive with laughter and fun,
As insects play until the new dawn's begun.
In the fields where the shadows take flight,
Who knew bugs could bring such delight?

Beneath the Shadowed Arches

Under arches where the trees entwine,
A squirrel finds a hidden stash of pine.
He thinks it's gold, a treasure he'll keep,
While other critters giggle and peep.

Badger joins with a stack of sweet dirt,
Claiming it's cake, no chance of hurt.
With crumbs on his nose, he takes a proud stance,
In this absurd woodland, all join the dance.

A hedgehog escapes from a grumpy old troll,
With a jolly old hat, he plays a role.
He rolls and he tumbles, much to our surprise,
There's laughter and joy in those quirk-filled eyes.

The trees sway gently as night settles in,
With critters still bickering, they laugh with a grin.
A lively commotion where shadows conspire,
Together they weave a warmth full of fire.

Charms of the Forgotten Glade

In a glade where squirrels dance,
A chubby raccoon takes a chance.
He tries to climb a tree so tall,
But slips and grabs a twig—oh, fall!

A rabbit hops, with style so grand,
While mushrooms form a dancing band.
A snail moves slow, a tortoise too,
They gossip about the skies so blue.

The owls wear glasses, looking wise,
While fireflies light up the night skies.
A fox in socks struts down the lane,
He stops to play the ukulele—oh, what a pain!

So if you wander in this place,
Expect some laughter, a friendly face.
Just pack some snacks, and you might find,
Some woodland friends, who are quite blind.

Tapestry of Twisted Vine

The vines are tangled, oh what a scene,
A cat with hats, in shades of green.
He complains to the bugs, all buzzing around,
About how he lost his favorite crown.

A bear wearing sandals walks in a trance,
While frogs on lilies try to prance.
One frog slips off, with a mighty splash,
While dragonflies buzz, with a zesty flash.

A raccoon, dressed up, puts on a show,
He juggles acorns, look at him go!
The audience cheers, all critters and more,
But the grand finale? He trips out the door!

In this twisty maze, laughter will wind,
Where nature's quirks leave joy behind.
Just follow the giggles, the trails of fun,
In this verdant realm, the joy's never done.

Nature's Jewel Box

Upon a rock, a toad sings out loud,
While a proud peacock struts, oh-so-proud.
In this gem-filled space, so rich and rare,
Even the hedgehogs have flair to spare.

A chipmunk schemes with a nut in tow,
He plans a splash in the creek below.
"Just watch!" he squeaks, with a wink and grin,
He leaps and—whoosh!—Into the swirl he spins.

The clouds wear hats, fashioned by bees,
While lizards lounge, enjoying the breeze.
A witty crow tells tales that delight,
Of midnight feasts and the moon's soft light.

In this dazzling box, nature delights,
Full of treasures and silly sights.
So join this romp, get lost in the joy,
Where every day becomes a playful ploy.

The Canopy's Cradle

In the cradle of trees, where giggles reside,
A squirrel in pajamas slides down with pride.
With a cheeky grin and a leap so spry,
He lands on a branch—oh, my oh my!

A sloth with a snack hangs upside-down,
While monkeys spin tales, they never frown.
Each story told—oh, how they tease!
With a popcorn shower from the teasing breeze.

Beneath the canopy, shadows play tricks,
As shadows of owls give sly little kicks.
They hoot and they holler, in marvelous jest,
As the forest joins in, feeling quite blessed.

So venture beneath this leafy embrace,
With laughter and fun in every space.
In the cradle of giants, find joy and cheer,
For nature's funny antics draw us all near.

Forest Fragments and Memories

In the woods, a squirrel stole my hat,
Jumping branches like a acrobat.

Leaves play tag with the breeze today,
Whispering secrets in a merry way.

A raccoon with a grin, oh what a sight,
Dancing in moonbeams, stealing the night.

Footprints in mud lead to a chase,
Everyone's laughing, a wild race!

The Song of the Saw

The saw sings loudly, a tuneful cheer,
Chopping the wood without any fear.

Logs rolling downhill, a lumberjack's jest,
Barking orders like a giddy guest.

Chopping and laughing in rhythmic delight,
As trees play peekaboo, out of sight.

Saw dust is flying, a flurry of fun,
Under the sun, our work is never done!

Twilight Wonders in the Woods

As twilight falls, shadows start to dance,
Frogs in tuxedos, taking their chance.

Fireflies flicker, a party so bright,
Buzzing around, all through the night.

Owls hoot out jokes with wise old flair,
Pointing fingers at those unaware.

Branches sway gently, playing a tune,
Nature's own disco, beneath the moon!

A Tapestry of Bark and Branch

Cacti in costumes, what a strange sight,
Thinking they're trees, it's a leafy fright.

Bark like a blanket, fuzzy and stout,
Squirrels knitting tales, never a doubt.

Branches are arms waving hello,
Inviting us in for the evening show.

Trees giggle softly, rustling with glee,
Nature's a theater, oh can't you see?

Beneath the Boughs of Time

Underneath the leafy crown,
Squirrels chatter, run, and frown.
Lost their acorns, oh what a mess,
Now they're left with brunch distress!

Beneath branches, secrets lie,
A raccoon plans a pie up high.
With sticky paws and dreaming eyes,
He hopes for fruit and a big surprise!

Tickling breezes, whispers pass,
A rabbit's hope for leafy grass.
Bathing in sun, a lizard grins,
All while the clumsy deer trips and spins!

Time sways on a hammock's swing,
Nature's laughter starts to ring.
Plenty of giggles in forest cheer,
Beneath the boughs, fun is near!

Woodland Whimsy and Wonder

A hedgehog in a bowler hat,
Dances with a smiling cat.
Mushrooms twirl in laughter bold,
Sharing secrets to be told!

A fox with shades, stylish and sly,
Pretends to be a super spy.
Beneath the twigs, the beetles groove,
Making up steps for their silly move!

Here comes a turtle playing drums,
Beating hearts and making thumps.
Snails cheer in their shiny shells,
Making music from tiny bells!

Waves of fun in sunlight's glow,
Creatures gather, put on a show.
Gloriously whimsical, wild, and free,
The forest bursts with jubilee!

Stories Suspended in Air

A heron tells a tale of flight,
While a gust gives him quite a fright.
"Did you see me sky-surf down?
I almost dropped my fancy crown!"

Clouds join in with chuckles loud,
As silly owls gather around.
One says, "Who?" and all agree,
Mistakes are made quite frequently!

Breezes gossip, tickling leaves,
Whispering secrets that nobody believes.
A bear in shades, lounging around,
Claims he's "Paw-some" in this crowd!

From roots to roosts, tales take flight,
Under stars in the velvet night.
Nature's laughter fills the air,
Stories shared, beyond compare!

Footprints on Forgotten Trails

Once a pig trod a muddy track,
Now he's stuck, no turning back.
A chicken struts, quite unimpressed,
Laughs out loud and feels blessed!

On paths untamed, each stumble's fun,
Muddy footprints make a run.
Raccoons giggle at every fall,
As clumsy creatures prance and sprawl!

Old stones whisper of days gone by,
While laughter echoes, oh my, oh my!
A squirrel juggles at the bend,
All their antics never end!

Celebrating every twist and turn,
In woods where friendship's cool and warm.
Footprints left, a playful reel,
Adventures linger, that's the deal!

www.ingramcontent.com/pod-product-compliance
Lightning Source LLC
Chambersburg PA
CBHW072147200426
43209CB00051B/820